CEZANNE

Elizabeth Elias Kaufman

CASTLE
BOOKS

A Division of
BOOK SALES, INC.
110 Enterprise Avenue
Secaucus, N.J. 07094

ISBN: 0-89009-371-7

CONTENTS

COLOR ILLUSTRATIONS

CEZANNE

Cézanne, master of still life, landscape, and portraiture, was one of the least understood artists of his time. His art shocked and disgusted the ruling art world. Critics claimed the distortions in his paintings proved that he couldn't even draw. At one time or another, his vile temper, shyness, and lonely temperament alienated every one of his friends and supporters. Few people knew him well. Even fewer ever penetrated his protective shell. During his lifetime, he never achieved the fame his art deserved. Yet, today, he is recognized as a master artist whose work laid the foundations for Cubism. Many of his problems were a result of the times in which he lived. To understand Cézanne, one must examine the state of art in nineteenth century France.

HIS TIMES

Art during the nineteenth century was not limited to any one movement or style. Rather, art movements arrived in waves. To continue the analogy, the movements built slowly, peaked, and entered a slow period of decline. Romanticism was eventually replaced by Realism. Impressionism overtook Realism. Post-Impressionism followed Impressionism. However, as is true with most art movements, the change was gradual. Warring schools vied for attention. Styles were not born nor did they die overnight. Thus, an artist such as Cézanne was exposed to several styles at any given time. Each style was the expression of a different philosophy of art.

At the beginning of the nineteenth century, the dominant movement was Romanticism. However, there was still a large number of artists who could be described as followers of Neoclassicism, and there was still more than a trace of the ornate Baroque movement and the controlled elegance of the Rococo in art. Romantics centered their attention on nature, adventure, and romance. Many of Cézanne's early works are Romantic in nature, with titles such as *The Rape* and *The Orgy*. Artists of this school produced highly emotional works utilizing color to a much greater degree than the somewhat subdued Neoclassical artists did.

The new art movement was Realism. Unlike the Romantics, these artists depended on their experiences. Since none of them had ever seen an angel, it was impossible for them to paint one. Unless you had been to a forest, you didn't paint a forest. Led by Gustave Courbet, the Realists caused a tremendous stir. Their art was not necessarily pleasant, showed no imaginative flights of fancy, and was considered undignified.

In 1863, Edouard Manet painted *Le Dejeuner Sur l'Herbe (Luncheon on the Grass)*. This piece is often thought of as the first Impressionistic painting. Although it is an early work, it contains many of the characteristics that were later associated with Impressionism. If Courbet and the Realists caused a stir, Manet and the early Impressionists caused an uproar.

The name of this new art movement, Impressionism, was adopted from the title of a painting by Claude Monet, *Impression: Sunrise*. The Impressionists broke a tradition that had begun during the Renaissance. They concentrated on color and light, more or less abandoning the use of chiaroscuro (the interplay of light and dark). The few shadows found in Impressionistic works were generally achieved through the use of deeper colors rather than the browns and blacks. The emphasis on color and light, the elimination of most details, and the infrequent use of lines resulted in somewhat flat images.

The reality of the visual experience was all important to the Impressionists. Rather than attempting to make religious, moral, or political statements, these artists frequently painted landscapes. The title of this movement indicates one of the reasons the art establishment reacted so violently to it. Art was not supposed to represent an impression. It was supposed to make a statement, tell a story, or illustrate an event.

The most obvious characteristic of this style is the short brushstroke. This was used to give the painting a shimmering quality similar to the natural effect of light hitting an object. It was also used in an attempt to complete the work as quickly as possible before the light shifted and changed the visual experience.

There was no clear-cut movement following Impressionism. The rather vague term, "Post-Impressionism", is used to cover a broad range of styles that followed Impressionism. There were, however, two characteristics that the Post-Impressionists shared. First, like the Impressionists, these artists were interested in the effects of color and light; and second, they attempted to solidify the structures and forms used in their art.

In France at this time, the art world was controlled by the Academy of Fine Arts. Through its official exhibition of new works, the Salon, the Academy dictated public tastes. Only officially approved styles were accepted for exhibition. An artist whose works were rejected by the Academy for the Salon could expect only limited success. However, by 1863, there was so much anger and discontent among the rejected artists, that something had to be done. In May of 1863, the government sponsored a separate exhibition, the Salon des Refusés. Held in the Palais de l'Industrie, the exhibition was open to any artist whose works had been rejected by the Academy's Salon. Many of the early Impressionists first exhibited this way.

Although the power and popularity of the Impressionists weakened the control of the Academy of Fine Arts, artists were still not totally free to do as they wanted; at least not if they wanted to earn a living through their art. Even within the rebel group, artists were expected to exhibit a certain degree of conformity. Thus, there were limits to the amount of eccentricity that was tolerated. Unfortunately, Cézanne frequently overstepped the accepted boundaries. Like many other great artists, he had his own vision of what was right and proper in art. Although he knew and associated with many of the other master artists of his time, he seldom agreed with them. As a result, both socially and artistically, he was always on the fringe of the group that had begun as rebels and ended as accepted artists.

HIS LIFE

Paul Cézanne was born on January 19, 1839 in the small French town of Aix-en-Provence. He was the only son of Louis-Auguste Cézanne and Anne-Elisabeth-Honorine Aubert. His father was an extremely clever and ambitious man who started as an apprentice in the millinery business and who eventually opened his own bank. His mother had worked for the senior Cézanne and had been his mistress for several years before they married.

Cézanne was brought up on a large estate his father had purchased. Called *Le Jas de* *Bouffan* (plate 19), the manor house was a home to which he returned frequently during much of his adult life. The town itself was a quiet, rural backwater.

During his childhood, he formed a friendship with Émile Zola that lasted many years and was to become an important part of Cézanne's life and career. The two young men, along with Baptistin Baille, shared a happy boyhood. Cézanne and Zola thought of themselves as intellectuals. Both intended to become writers.

Cézanne was a good student. He seemed

to have a natural facility for languages such as Latin and Greek. Along with his academic subjects, he took drawing lessons. Although he showed an interest in art, he had no special ability at this time. In fact, his friend Émile Zola was a better artist as a boy.

Even as a child, Cézanne was moody and capable of violent emotional swings. His personality was probably the result of his home life. It is a familiar pattern, a domineering father, an overly protective mother. Whatever the cause, the result was an unstable and unhappy personality.

In 1858, Zola moved to Paris. Both young men enjoyed corresponding. In his letters, Cézanne revealed his feelings towards women. He was both attracted and repelled by them. His problems in this area were severe. It was not until he was thirty that he formed a true relationship with a woman.

With his friend Zola in Paris, Cézanne finished his high school work and continued his drawing lessons. In the fall, he entered law school. He had no desire to study law, but his father insisted. For several years, he struggled at the law school of the University of Aix. Finally, he decided he wanted to become a painter. With his mother's help, he secured his father's permission to drop out of law school.

Early in 1861, Cézanne's father allowed him to go to Paris to become a painter, giving his son enough money to support himself.

Knowing that he was not qualified to be accepted at the prestigious Academy of Fine Arts, Cézanne tried to prepare himself by attending the Atelier Suisse. He also spent a lot of time in the Louvre. He worked hard, but he was no match for his contemporaries. Unlike some master artists, he was not born with a perfected style or a mature talent; he had to develop his skills. A few months after arriving in Paris, Cézanne returned to Aix in despair. His visits to the Louvre had been the only positive experience of his short lived stay in Paris.

For approximately a year, Cézanne remained in Aix, working in his father's bank, hating every minute of it. At the same time, he resumed his drawing lessons. In the fall of 1862, Cézanne decided to return to Paris. Evi-

dently his father agreed, for he is known to have given his son money.

At the age of twenty-three, Cézanne returned to Paris and the Atelier Suisse. He applied to the Academy of Fine Arts, but was not accepted. Apparently his determination to become a painter was strong enough to withstand this rejection and the countless others that followed, for he never returned to the bank.

For most of the rest of the decade, Cézanne worked in Paris. The pattern of frequently returning home continued. In 1863, he exhibited in the Salon des Refusés. That was the year Manet's **Luncheon on the Grass** created such an uproar. It is doubtful that Cézanne's paintings were very noticeable, because he was still producing Romantic works. In any event, it is not known which of his pieces were exhibited at the 1863 Salon des Refusés.

Although he knew and associated with many of the leading artists, Cézanne was never truly at ease with them, nor was he totally accepted by them. His rough dress, heavy accent, crude language, and boorish behavior alienated most people. The one exception was Pissarro, who would later have a tremendous impact on his art.

In 1869, he met Marie-Hortense Fiquet. She was more than a decade younger than Cézanne, and the first and only female with whom he had a lasting relationship. She was his mistress for seventeen years. He finally married her in 1886. Although it endured, the relationship was strange; they frequently spent more time apart than together.

1872 was an important year in Cézanne's life. His son, Paul was born in January. Later in the year, Cézanne and his new family went to live and work with Pissarro in Pontoise. This older artist was both father and teacher to Cézanne. He helped Cézanne understand the importance of color and taught him how to apply the elements of Impressionism. The outdoor painting and life in the countryside agreed with Cézanne. His mature style began to emerge as a result of Pissarro's tutoring.

Cézanne's work, although influenced by Pissarro, was different. He wanted to combine the emphasis on color stressed by the Impressionists with the form and solidity found in the art of the old masters. The application of geometry helped him to accomplish this. Eventually, he saw nature in terms of three basic geometric shapes: the cylinder, the cone, and the sphere.

It was not until 1895 that he began to achieve fame. In that year Ambroise Vollard, the influential art dealer, exhibited Cézanne's work. Although other artists began to understand the importance of his art, the general public refused to accept Cézanne.

Cézanne continued to work near his home, painting an entire series of a mountain near there, **Mont Sainte-Victoire** (plate 42). He died on October 22, 1906 at the age of sixty-seven, an artistic genius whose works were not fully appreciated at the time.

HIS WORKS

PLATE 1

Cézanne worked on this portrait of his *Uncle Dominique as a Monk* from 1865 until 1867. It is fairly typical of the artist's early works. The paint has been applied very heavily, the subject is visualized as dark and brooding, and the work lacks the technical finesse Cézanne acquired in his later years.

During this early period, Cézanne painted quite a number of portraits of his uncle. As was the case with most of his early work, the paintings exhibited an uncontrolled savage fury. *Uncle Dominique as a Monk* reveals the influence of the Romantics at this point in Cézanne's career.

PLATE 2

While he was working on *Uncle Dominique as a Monk* (plate 1), Cézanne painted this *Portrait of Louis-Auguste Cézanne,* his father. None of his wildly conflicting emotions towards his father appear in the portrait. This could be any man reading the newspaper. The colors are very dark, as was typical of works he produced at the time. Even at this early stage, Cézanne was using geometry in composing his paintings. The strong line of the wall is paralleled by the rigidly rectangular shape of the chair. The small painting behind the chair is thought to be one of Cézanne's first still life compositions.

PLATE 3

The Black Clock, painted between 1869 and 1871, is an early still life. Nevertheless, it is a masterpiece. The perfect balance of the piece is the result of both the use of geometry and the controlled application of color.

Cézanne balanced the darkness of the clock with the red of the shell lips. The colors of the shell, the lemon, and the vase on top of the clock play off of each other and are in turn balanced by the alternating black and white of the cloth on the table.

The scalloped edge of the tall glass vase echoes the top of the shell. Behind the vase is a fluted column. Cézanne used the stark shape of the clock to control and balance these curves. Notice that the clock has no hands. Because Cézanne gave no clues as to the reason for this, the viewer is left pondering the significance of a clock without hands.

PLATE 4

In order to avoid being drafted during the war years, Cézanne and his mistress moved to the small city of L'Estaque. In later years, he painted other scenes of the area in his mature style. However, in *Melting Snow at L'Estaque,* Cézanne was still using a Romantic approach to landscape painting. The work is violent, gloomy, and visually disturbing. The focus of the painting forms a triangular wedge which is fitted into the steeply banked hillside and the ominous sky.

PLATE 5

Pissarro's influence on Cézanne is obvious in **The Cottage in the Trees.** Although painted only a few years after **Melting Snow at L'Estaque** (plate 4), this painting is executed in an entirely different style. From Pissarro, Cézanne learned the elements of Impressionism and how to apply them. In contrast to his earlier work, Cézanne concentrated on the use of color and light in **The Cottage in the Trees.** The emotional intensity of his earlier style is missing. Cézanne was beginning to learn to control and channel his energy.

PLATE 6

A Modern Olympia, painted in 1873, was a humorous allusion to Edouard Manet's earlier work, **Olympia.** Cézanne's painting was ridiculed and scorned when it was exhibited in 1874, much as Manet's original piece had been. The work is light and airy and obviously painted by an artist with a sense of humor. Because of the humor, it is atypical of Cézanne, who took his art very seriously.

The playful, yet erotic nature of the work was viewed as an assault on traditional art. The painting itself shows a sensuous nude being uncovered before the eyes of a man of means. It has a definite Romantic quality, although the gloom and violence found in Cézanne's earlier Romantic works are not evident here.

PLATE 7

Just as Cézanne was slow to reach his mature style, he was also a very slow worker. As a result, he often preferred working with stable subjects such as still life compositions. Cézanne worked on this **Delft Vase with Dahlias** from 1873 until 1875.

The prolonged study and painting time was at odds with the way the Impressionists approached their work. Nevertheless, **Delft Vase with Dahlias** has definite Impressionistic elements. At this point in his career, Cézanne was beginning to work more with color than he had before.

PLATE 8

Victor Chocquet was a government worker who developed a passion for modern art. In addition to being a great admirer of Renoir's work, he was one of the first people to recognize and support Cézanne's talents.

Portrait of Chocquet was painted in 1875 and exhibited in 1877. Like all of Cézanne's work at the time, it was severely criticized. Although the art public was beginning to accept Impressionism, they were not prepared to deal with Cézanne's style. Here, he has shown the art patron turned to one side, accentuating the subject's contemplative nature. Cézanne's portrait has a solidity of structure that separated his work from that of many of the Impressionists. The brushstrokes and modeling of the head itself, the features, and even Chocquet's hair give the painting a dynamic rhythm and flow.

PLATE 9

The Walls was painted during the same period that Cézanne was working on his **Portrait of Chocquet** (plate 8). Both paintings have a rhythm and flow that keep the viewer's eye moving.

Here, Cézanne used short brushstrokes in some areas to achieve a dappled, sunlit effect, characteristic of the Impressionists. However, compared with Cézanne's paintings, other Impressionistic works appear almost flat. Cézanne has given this piece tremendous depth. Unlike some of his later works, he was still using browns and blacks to create shadows and depth. Notice the way the trunks of the trees are outlined in dark colors. In this painting, the viewer can begin to see elements of Cézanne's more mature style.

PLATE 10

At the time Cézanne was painting **Houses and Trees in Provence,** he was spending almost all of his time in the area. He was frequently seen tramping around the countryside with his canvas and easel.

This piece exhibits the perfect balance for which Cézanne is famous. The touches of red are controlled by the greens. The large building on the left is countered with several small buildings on the right. Also evident in the work is Cézanne's reliance on geometry. Notice that each of the buildings has been reduced to blocks and planes.

PLATE 11

By the time Cézanne painted **The Bridge of Maincy,** he was approaching his mature style. He was beginning to see all of nature in terms of cylinders, cones, and spheres. His use of color distinguishes this painting from his more mature style. He was still using color only to show the effects of light. Later, color would become the vehicle for definition and structure.

The reflections in **The Bridge of Maincy** are a good example of the way Cézanne altered the visual reality to meet the needs and purposes of his art. Instead of a mirror image, Cézanne reflects only that which will enhance the total picture.

PLATE 12

Medea is a watercolor interpretation of a similar painting by Delacroix. According to Greek mythology, **Medea** was responsible for helping Jason win the Golden Fleece. When he deserted her, Medea killed her children, set the palace on fire, and fled. She is shown here with the knife in her hand after having murdered her children.

Delacroix's art was important to Cézanne. He adopted the older artist's technique of using color rather than line as the controlling factor in a picture. This "composition by color" is most evident in Cézanne's still life work such as **Still Life with Basket of Pears** (plate 29) and **Still Life with Basket of Apples** (plate 33).

PLATE 13

The landscape entitled **Road Leading to a Lake** contains good examples of the effectiveness of Cézanne's brushstroke technique. He used short brushstrokes (like the Impressionists) applied on a diagonal. The angle of the brushstroke provides tremendous movement. It also balances the piece. Notice that the angle of the brushstrokes helps to soften the rather severe vertical lines of the trees. The horizontal angle of the brushstrokes on the road seems to widen it, and also helps balance the vertical lines. The horizontal lines in the middle of the painting help to visually widen the piece. Finally, Cézanne uses the tops of the trees, the undergrowth, and the mound on the right-hand side to dampen the effects of the horizontal and vertical planes.

PLATE 14

Cézanne painted many of the scenes around Pontoise. He worked on this one from 1879 until 1882. **The Mill at Pontoise** provides an interesting contrast to his earlier work, **Melting Snow at L'Estaque** (plate 4). By the time he painted **The Mill at Pontoise,** Cézanne had learned to control and direct his intensity. **Melting Snow at L'Estaque** is a moody, gloomy piece. Cézanne's personal involvement with the painting is very obvious. This is not the case with **The Mill at Pontoise.** It appears to have been painted more with the eyes and head than with the heart. In fact, this change of focus from emotion to intellect is one of the characteristics that distinguishes the artist's later works.

PLATE 15

The *Portrait of Louis Guillaume* reveals more about the artist than about the subject. Louis Guillaume was the son of a friend. He was an unremarkable young man. Cézanne modeled the face in a rather strange way. A careful examination shows that the boy's face has three planes representing the eyes, the nose, and the chin. Despite the distortion, the face appears to be correct. This device causes the eye to move down the face to the scarf to the motif on the wall and back to the face again.

PLATE 16

Even as a young man, Cézanne appeared to be older than he was. In 1879, when this *Self-Portrait* was started, he was only forty years old, yet he appears to be a good deal older than that. Although Cézanne painted many self-portraits, this is probably the most famous. Notice that in this portrait, as in the *Portrait of Louis Guillaume* (plate 15), Cézanne does not try to capture the subject's personality. Because of this, his portraits are often compared with his still life compositions. This one is constructed of pure geometric shapes. The triangular pattern in the wallpaper is repeated in the lapel of his coat. The circle of his features is surrounded by his beard to form an oval or cylinder.

PLATE 17

With the exception of his early work, Cézanne did not usually employ figures in his landscapes. However, beginning in about 1880, he attempted to unite landscape and the human form as elements of nature. With *Bacchanal* (also known as *The Battle of Love*), Cézanne combined elements of Impressionism with Romanticism, utilizing a classical theme. The title and the painting do not quite match. The image is more of a rape scene than a classical battle of love. In later years, Cézanne executed a series of paintings involving bathers which bear some similarity to this piece, but which are technically superior.

PLATE 18

Cézanne's fame as an artist rests partially on the perfect harmony and balance he achieved in his art. *Seascape at L'Estaque* is an example of this ability. The view from above gives the viewer the impression of looking at a model. Each element of the painting is carefully placed. This meticulous planning occurred during the actual application of paint. It is said that Cézanne would frequently pause for lengthy periods of time, thoughtfully debating the wisdom of one minute brushstroke. The result is that each stroke is correct in the same way that each element in the painting is correct in size, angle, and placement.

PLATE 19

Le Jas de Bouffan was the manor house Louis-Auguste Cézanne owned. Cézanne returned there frequently at the time this piece was painted. Although he obviously had intense emotional feelings towards the house and the time he spent there, this work was executed with an almost clinical detachment. Nothing has been romanticized. The house itself is seen through the trees and shrubbery. The roof, walls, and windows are architectural blocks fitted together to form a solid whole. The colors of the roof are echoed in the gardens directly in front of the house and to the left of the house.

PLATE 20

In his still life compositions, Cézanne used many of the same techniques he utilized in painting landscapes. As a result, works such as *Pot of Flowers on a Table* have the same monumental quality that the artist's landscape work has.

This piece exhibits several of the characteristics for which Cézanne was so severely criticized. Notice that the work has several perspectives. The background is seen from a different angle than the foreground. Additionally, Cézanne deliberately distorted the lip of the jug. This was done to balance the protruding brush handle. The pattern of the jug echoes the line of the lip. A similar distortion is obvious in the rim of the dish. Cézanne used these distortions to balance the work. Unfortunately, at the time, art critics were unable to understand or to see the brilliance of his work.

PLATE 21

The table in *Still Life with Soup Tureen* has been tilted towards the viewer. This serves two purposes. It exposes more of the surface. It also reinforces the flat quality of the still life to counterbalance the depth Cézanne wanted to include. The opposition of depth and flatness is characteristic of Cézanne.

The artist was a master at painting fruit. Each apple shows the careful, painstaking work for which Cézanne is famous. The detail work in the apples provided by slight color variations is extraordinary. These same color variations are used in the soup tureen.

PLATE 22

The Blue Vase is one of Cézanne's most famous still life paintings. It is also an excellent example of the way Cézanne used color as a structural element in addition to its decorative function. Here, he has used a wide range of variations in blue to help build his composition. The entire work is so perfectly balanced that the viewer must take a second look in order to find the distortions that create the balance. The structural lines (including the diagonal behind the vase) are countered with the imaginative floral arrangement. The two apples on the right balance the partially obscured bottle on the left. Notice that the two apples are not complete. Their unfinished state keeps them in a subsidiary position. Finally, Cézanne has restated the curved edge of the vase in the scalloped border of the plate behind it.

PLATE 23

Cézanne's use of diagonal brushstrokes in the tops of the trees gives *The Viaduct* a windy feel. This is one of the few landscapes produced at the time with this kind of movement. Normally, Cézanne's scene is static; the sense of motion is caused by the angle of the brushstrokes and by the composition. The viaduct from which the painting takes its title was often used by Cézanne. In the background to the left is Mont Sainte-Victoire. In this piece, it is barely visible and is only a secondary element. However, in later years, Cézanne was fascinated by the mountain and painted it scores of times such as *Mont Sainte-Victoire, View from the Southwest* (plate 35).

PLATE 24

The artist worked on the *Portrait of Madame Cézanne* from 1885 until 1887. During this period, Cézanne married Hortense. Although they spent a great deal of time separated from each other, Cézanne painted quite a few portraits of her. With most of his portraits, Cézanne approached the work as he might a still life or landscape. However, this painting is not totally devoid of emotion. The portrait gives the viewer an idea of the subject's personality. Cézanne has given the face a sad, slightly petulant quality.

PLATE 25

One of the areas of controversy among scholars of Cézanne's work is whether or not *View of Gardanne* is a finished piece. Cézanne often left parts of his work unfinished in order to emphasize other elements. In this case, the incomplete nature of the bottom right-hand corner forces the eye up and to the right. This is the natural sweep of the work. The houses on the right are arranged as steps leading the eye up to the unfinished tower.

PLATE 26

Geometric elements are very obvious in *Mountains in Provence.* This is especially true in the fields and buildings in the background. In the foreground, the geometry is not as obvious. The rocks are painted to suggest the way a village might appear when seen from a distance. In fact, the red roof in the background is seen as reflected light on the rocks. The painting is suffused with sunlight. Paintings such as *Mountains in Provence* exerted a tremendous influence on later artists. The Cubists in particular owed a great deal to Cézanne.

PLATE 27

During the latter part of the 1880's, Cézanne painted four oils and a watercolor that bear no real relationship to his other work at the time. The pieces revolve around the theme of the Harlequin. *Mardi Gras,* painted in 1888, also includes the pathetic clown, Pierrot. The source of the inspiration for these works is unknown. One theory suggests that Cézanne, who was living in Paris at the time, was involved in some way with the circus. Given his temperament, that is highly unlikely.

Cézanne used his teenage son, Paul, as his model for the Harlequin. Louis Guillaume, whose portrait Cézanne had earlier painted (plate 15), was the model for Pierrot. It is believed that this series was part of the inspiration for Picasso's use of the Harlequin in his Rose Period and in his later works.

PLATE 28

Road at Chantilly was painted in 1888. It is unusual in that the view is very limited. Cézanne's landscapes tend to be somewhat freer. In this work, he gives the observer a very narrow channel. In fact, the viewer can't be sure if he is looking at one building or at several. Cézanne united the work through his use of color. The color in the foreground is reflected in the walls. The roof colors are also seen in the trees. The strong vertical line of the trees is balanced by the lines of the roof and by the barrier in the road.

PLATE 29

Cézanne's skill with still life is evident in *Still Life with Basket of Pears.* This is one of his most complex paintings. Each element has been placed and painted with attention to detail and with regard for the work as a whole. What appears to be an asymmetrical design is actually very subtly balanced. Several of the elements in the piece have been distorted to help achieve this balance. The table on which the basket rests is clearly distorted. The legs don't match, the two front edges are uneven and on different planes, and the top of the table is also on two planes. Additionally, the legs of the chair in the background are not the same.

PLATES 30, 31

Together these two plates form *The Card Players.* Cézanne painted five versions of this piece. In the others, the number of subjects ranges up to five. In some there are onlookers. This is the last of the five versions, and considered by many to be the best. The piece itself has no action and tells no story. Cézanne used contrasts to achieve a monumental quality. Both men appear to be contemplative; however, the two figures are opposites. The figure to the left (plate 30) is calm and relaxed. His clothes are neat, he wears a fairly formal hat, and his back is straight. On the other hand, the figure on the right (plate 31) appears to be unsure of his next move, his clothes are rumpled, his hat bent and informal, and his back and shoulders arch towards the cards. Even the angle of the tablecloth is different in front of each player. In order to balance the fuller, more intense figure on the right, Cézanne shifted the entire scene to the right. This move gives equal weight to both players.

PLATE 32

The stark lines of the table and floor in *Pitcher of Milk, Apples, and Lemon* are softened by the fruit, pitcher, and dish. As he often did in still life works, Cézanne tilted the top of the table towards the viewer. In this case, the angle is such that the top of the table almost faces the viewer. The angle of the floor is also distorted, providing a strong diagonal line. Although the composition is not as complex as *Still Life with Basket of Pears* (plate 29), it has the same sense of perfect balance.

PLATE 33

This detail from *Still Life with Basket of Apples* represents the upper left-hand quarter of the painting. Cézanne worked on the piece from 1890 until 1894. Each piece of fruit is a masterpiece, shaped and textured by color

alone. An incredible number of brushstrokes was needed to achieve this result. Even in this detail, Cézanne's ability to use distortion for balance is obvious. Both the basket and the bottle are irregular, yet the effect is harmonious and pleasing.

PLATE 34

The Forest is one of many watercolors Cézanne created. Beginning in about 1890, he used this medium frequently. In this piece, Cézanne's masterful use of color helps to balance the fascinating line of trees. It is curious that an artist who required so much time to finish an oil painting would be interested in watercolor work. This medium allows for no corrections, permits no mistakes. Nevertheless, Cézanne mastered the technique in works such as *The Forest* and *The River at the Bridge of the Three Springs* (plate 48).

PLATE 35

Cézanne painted approximately sixty views of Mont Sainte-Victoire. This one, *Mont Sainte-Victoire, View from the Southwest* was painted during the 1890's. The mountain near his home fascinated, even obsessed him. In this painting, Cézanne was working on an interesting perspective. The mountain appears to be both near and far off. This highly complex work has been executed with a deceptive simplicity.

PLATE 36

The focus of *Still Life with Peppermint Bottle* is the flask next to the bottle. This painting shows Cézanne's unique talents with still life compositions. In the flask one can see both the reflection of the glass in front of it, and the image of the fruit behind it. Notice the way the strong vertical and horizontal lines of the wall are balanced by the round shape of the bottle and the graceful curves of the flask.

PLATE 37

Cézanne's housekeeper was the model for the **Woman with Coffee Pot.** Posing for Cézanne was always a problem. He insisted that his models remain absolutely motionless, sometimes for hours at a time.

The artist used curved lines in the woman's dress to emphasize her found figure. The softness is played against the lines in the door behind her. Notice how the coffee pot and the spoon in the cup parallel the lines in the door.

PLATE 38

Still Life with Plaster Cupid is one of two paintings Cézanne executed in which the same plaster cast is the focus of attention. The artist used the fruit on the table to echo the rounded shapes found in the cupid's body. The table on which these objects rest has been distorted into several planes. First, it is tilted towards the viewer, a technique Cézanne used frequently in his still life compositions. In addition, the right and left sides do not match. Finally, the left-hand corner of the table is higher than the right-hand corner.

PLATE 39

The Château Noir was a building near Aix. It had a somewhat strange shape that intrigued Cézanne. For a while, he had a studio in the building. He included it in several of his Mont Sainte-Victoire paintings. In this watercolor, **Pistachio Trees at the Château Noir,** the artist used the angle of the roof to balance the tree limbs. It is interesting to note that the trees in the background have leaves, but the trees in the foreground are bare.

PLATE 40

This portrait, **Peasant in a Blue Shirt,** was one of a number of portraits Cézanne painted at the time. He frequently used local workers as models. Unlike some of his earlier portraits, such as **Portrait of Louis Guillaume** (plate 15), this man's face is on a realistic plane. Behind the man's right shoulder, Cézanne painted the rough outline of a woman. She has no face. Above her head is a vague shape that could be a parasol or a mountain.

PLATE 41

Joachim Gasquet was the son of one of Cézanne's childhood friends. This portrait was painted in 1896, shortly after they met. For a while, he and Cézanne were good friends. However, as Cézanne had grown older, his personality had become more unstable. Eventually, he alienated Joachim Gasquet just as he had alienated all of his other friends.

PLATE 42

Cézanne painted this view of **Mont Sainte-Victoire** in 1900. Although his use of geometry is obvious, the painting is very complex. There are strong Impressionistic elements, but there is also an abstract quality. Both the composition and the colors are carefully balanced. The colors in the sky are reflected in the mountain and in the fields. Colors in the foreground are also seen in the background. Parts of the work appear to be unfinished. This is especially evident along the left-hand side of the painting.

PLATE 43

Woman with a Book shows a woman stylishly dressed. It is one of the few portraits in which the artist used this kind of costume. Cézanne was a master portrait painter; however, he had one flaw. He did not paint hands very well. The woman's hands here are too large and rough for the rest of the portrait. His problem in illustrating hands can also be seen in the clown's hand in *Mardi Gras* (plate 27) and *Woman with Coffee Pot* (plate 37).

One of the interesting aspects of *Woman with a Book* is the treatment of the drapery. Notice that the drapes become increasingly abstract as they pass the woman's shoulder.

PLATE 44

Painted in 1903, only three years before his death, *Blue Landscape,* although unfinished, gives the viewer a good idea of the direction towards which Cézanne was moving. His art became increasingly free and abstract. He continued to work outside, finding a suitable view and altering it to suit his artistic needs. Many photographs exist of the scenes Cézanne painted. They prove that his work was based on the scene as he viewed it.

PLATE 45

The simple scene of *Pines and Rocks* has a monumental quality. Part of Cézanne's genius was his ability to take a prosaic country view and turn it into a masterpiece. The colors are perfectly balanced here. The brighter colors are toned down by the cooler tones. Each element reflects the color found in other elements. The strong vertical lines formed by the tree trunks are played against the geometric shapes of the rocks and the wispy leaves.

PLATE 46

The watercolor known as *Apples, Bottle, and Chairback* is an excellent example of Cézanne's ability to work in this medium. This is not a sketch in preparation for a painting. It is a finished work. Considering the time and care involved in his paintings, it is amazing that Cézanne was able to use watercolors at all. The same elements that are found in his paintings are present here. The color of the glass is reflected in the dish, fruit, and table. The fanciful chairback frames the fruit dish and is echoed by the arrangement of the fruit.

PLATE 47

Mont Sainte-Victoire with the Château Noir is not complete. Its unfinished state gives the viewer an idea of Cézanne's watercolor technique. It is obvious that he first made a very rough sketch in pencil. It would appear that instead of working on one part of the piece at a time, he worked on one color at a time. This technique helped him balance the work from the beginning. In painting, he would add and subtract colors from different parts of the painting, but this is not possible when using watercolors.

PLATE 48

Cézanne executed this watercolor, *The River at the Bridge of the Three Springs* in 1906, the year he died. The delicate colors and free composition give it a very light feel. This work is the closest Cézanne ever came to total abstraction. The bridge appears to float across the sky. Cézanne used his colors and the bridge to balance the strong vertical line of the tree. From this work and others produced during the last few years of his life, it is clear that Cézanne was moving towards abstraction. Indeed, there is little doubt that modern art, especially Cubism, owes a great deal to Cézanne.

Plate 1 Uncle Dominique as a Monk, detail — his head,
1865-67, oil on canvas, private collection

Plate 2 Portrait of Louis-Auguste Cézanne, c. 1866, oil on
canvas, 6′ 6⅛″ X 3′ 11″, National Gallery of Art,
Washington, D.C.

Plate 3 The Black Clock, 1869-71, oil on canvas, 21⅝″ X 29⅛″,
Niarchos Collection, Paris

Plate 4 Melting Snow at L'Estaque, 1870-71, oil on canvas,
2′ 4¾′′ X 3′ ¼′′, Buhrle Collection, Zurich

Plate 5 The Cottage in the Trees, 1873, oil on canvas, 24″ X 19¾″,
courtesy of Durand-Ruel

Plate 6 A Modern Olympia, c. 1873, oil on canvas, 18⅛″ X 21⅝″,
Louvre, Paris

Plate 7 Delft Vase with Dahlias, 1873-75, oil on canvas, 28¾″ X 21¼″,
Louvre, Paris

23

Plate 8 Portrait of Chocquet, 1875, oil on canvas,
18⅛″ X 14⅛″, private collection

24

Plate 9 The Walls, 1875-76, oil on canvas, 20″ X 26″, courtesy
of Durand-Ruel

Plate 10 Houses and Trees in Provence, 1878-83, oil on canvas,
19⅝″ X 24″, National Gallery of Art, Washington, D.C.

Plate 11 The Bridge of Maincy, c. 1879-80, oil on canvas,
23″ X 28½″, Louvre, Paris

Plate 12 Medea, 1879-82, watercolor, 9¾″ X 14⅝″,
Kunsthaus, Zurich

Plate 13 Road Leading to a Lake, 1879-82, oil on canvas,
31⅞″ X 23⅝″, Kroller Muller Museum, Otterlo

29

Plate 14 The Mill at Pontoise, 1879-82, oil on canvas,
2′ 4¾′′ X 3′ ¼′′, Nationalgalerie, Berlin

Plate 15 Portrait of Louis Guillaume, 1879-82, oil on canvas,
22″ X 18⅛″, National Gallery of Art, Washington, D.C.   31

Plate 16 Self-Portrait, 1879-82, oil on canvas, 25⅝″ X 10⅝″,
National Gallery, London

Plate 17 Bacchanal, c. 1890, oil on canvas, 14⅞″ X 18½″,
National Gallery of Art, Washington, D.C.

Plate 18 Seascape at L'Estaque, 1882-85, oil on canvas,
2′ 1½″ X 2′ 8″, private collection

Plate 19 Le Jas de Bouffan, 1882-85, oil on canvas,
23¼″ X 28″, private collection

Plate 20 Pot of Flowers on a Table, 1882-87, oil on canvas,
23½″ X 28¾″, private collection

Plate 21 Still Life with Soup Tureen, 1883-85, oil on canvas,
2′ 1½″ X 2′ 8″, Louvre, Paris

Plate 22 The Blue Vase, 1883-87, oil on canvas, 24″ X 19⅝″,
Louvre, Paris

Plate 23 The Viaduct, 1885, oil on canvas, 2′ 11¾″ X 2′ 4⅛″,
Hermitage, Leningrad

Plate 24 Portrait of Madame Cézanne, 1885-87, oil on canvas,
18″ X 15″, private collection

Plate 25 View of Gardanne, 1885-86, oil on canvas, 3′ ¼″ X 2′ 4¾″,
Brooklyn Museum, Brooklyn

Plate 26 Mountains in Provence, 1886-90, oil on canvas,
2′ 1⅝″ X 2′ 7⅞″, National Gallery, London

Plate 27 Mardi Gras, 1888, oil on canvas, 3′ 3⅜′′ X 2′ 7⅞′′,
Hermitage, Leningrad

Plate 28 Road at Chantilly, 1888, oil on canvas,
2′ 7⅞″ X 2′ 1⅝″, private collection

Plate 29 Still Life with Basket of Pears, 1889-90, oil on canvas,
2′ 1⅝′′ X 2′ 7½′′, Louvre, Paris

Plate 30 The Card Players, detail — left figure, 1890-92,
oil on canvas, Louvre, Paris

Plate 31 The Card Players, detail — right figure

Plate 32 Pitcher of Milk, Apples, and Lemon, 1888-90, oil on
canvas, 28¾'' X 23⅝'', National Gallery, Oslo

Plate 33 Still Life with Basket of Apples, detail — basket and bottle,
1890-94, oil on canvas, The Art Institute of Chicago, Chicago

49

Plate 34 The Forest, 1890-1900, watercolor, 22⅜″ X 17⅛″,
The Newark Museum, Newark

Plate 35 Mont Sainte-Victoire, View from the Southwest,
1890-1900, oil on canvas, 2′ 7⅞″ X 3′ 3⅜″,
Hermitage, Leningrad

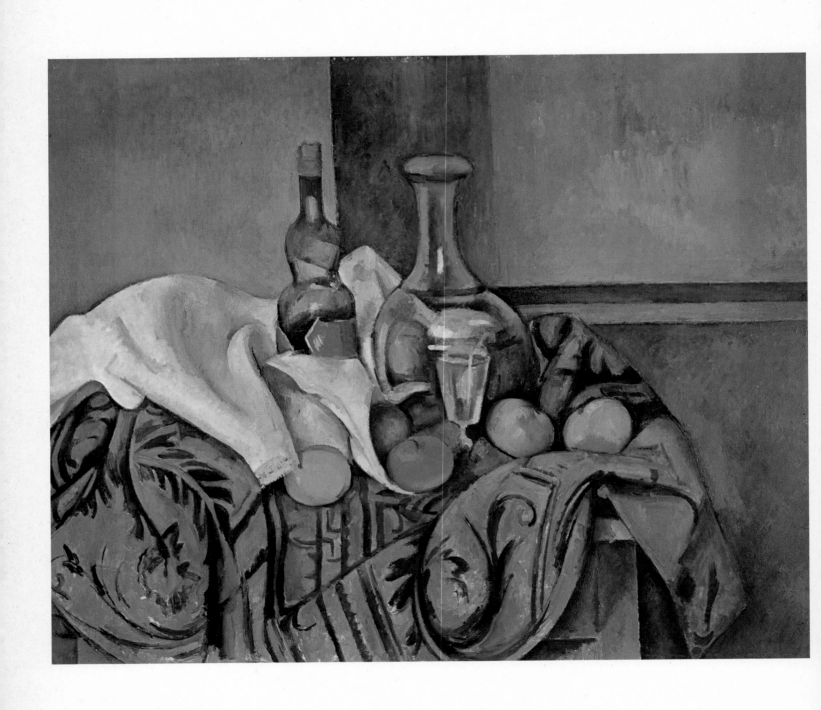

Plate 36 Still Life with Peppermint Bottle, 1894, oil on
canvas, National Gallery of Art, Washington, D.C.

Plate 37 Woman with Coffee Pot, c. 1895, oil on canvas,
4′ 3¼″ X 3′ 2¼″, Louvre, Paris

Plate 38 Still Life with Plaster Cupid, c. 1895, oil on canvas,
2′ ¾″ X 2′ 7¾″, National Museum, Stockholm

Plate 39 Pistachio Trees at the Château Noir, 1895-1900,
pencil and watercolor, 21″ X 16⅞″,
The Art Institute of Chicago, Chicago

Plate 40 Peasant in a Blue Shirt, 1895-1900, oil on canvas,
2′ 7⅞″ X 2′ 1⅝″, private collection

Plate 41 Joachim Gasquet, 1896, oil on canvas,
25⅝″ X 21¼″, Narodni Galerie, Prague

Plate 42 Mont Sainte-Victoire, 1900, oil on canvas,
2′ 6¾′′ X 3′ 3′′, Hermitage, Leningrad

Plate 43 Woman with a Book, 1900-04, oil on canvas,
25⅝″ X 19⅝″, private collection

Plate 44 Blue Landscape, c. 1903, oil on canvas,
3′ 4⅛″ X 2′ 8⅝″, Hermitage, Leningrad

Plate 45 Pines and Rocks, c. 1904, oil on canvas,
2′ 8″ X 2′ 1¾″, Museum of Modern Art, New York

Plate 46 Apples, Bottle, and Chairback, c. 1905, watercolor,
17½″ X 23¼″, Courtauld Institute of Art, London

Plate 47 Mont Sainte-Victoire with the Château Noir,
c. 1890-1906, pencil and watercolor,
12½″ X 19⅛″, Albertina, Vienna

63

Plate 48 The River at the Bridge of the Three Springs, 1906,
watercolor, 16″ X 21″, Cincinnati Art Museum,
Cincinnati